A Culture of Life

Women's theology and social liberation

CIIR Comment
by
Tina Beattie

GW00808743

About the author

Tina Beattie, a member of CIIR's Board of Trustees, teaches feminist theology and gender at the University of Bristol, and Wesley College, Bristol, and is a tutor counsellor with the Open University. She lived in Zambia, Zimbabwe and Kenya for many years.

Contents

Introduction: Women, justice and faith

It is not acceptable for women to constitute 70 per cent of the world's 1.3 billion absolute poor. Nor is it acceptable for women to work two-thirds of the world's working hours, but earn only one-tenth of the world's income and own less than one-tenth of the world's property. Many fundamental changes must be made.[1]

Gender and religion are significant factors in terms of human rights and economic development, but their influence tends to be ignored in analyses of poverty. For example, a recent United Nations report points out that 'None of the indicators commonly used to track the incidence and severity of income poverty are gender-sensitive.'[2] Although development agencies and non-governmental organisations (NGOs) are increasingly conscious of gender in their projects and campaigns, much remains to be done to assess the impact of poverty on women's lives.

Religious beliefs help to shape responses to poverty and injustice. When Karl Marx called religion 'the opium of the people' he was referring to its function in reconciling people to situations which would otherwise be intolerable. Religion can offer women a refuge which enables them to adapt to, rather than challenge, situations of oppression and violence, and it has conditioned women to accept positions of inferiority or subordination to men. However, that is only part of the story. The feminist historian Gerda Lerner describes how her research led her to recognise the positive influence of religion in women's struggles for freedom. She writes, 'The insight that religion was the primary arena on which women fought for hundreds of years for feminist consciousness was not one I had previously had.'[3] Religion is a potent factor in challenging as well as perpetuating injustice, and many women look to their religious traditions for the resources to inspire a more just social order.

This is a complex undertaking, for women have different views as to what constitutes the liberating potential of religion. For example, in El Salvador Catholic women drew on the insights of feminist and liberation theology to inform their resistance to violence during the civil war of

1980-92, in which some 75,000 people died. In East Timor after the Indonesian invasion, a conservative form of Catholicism gave women the personal strength to persevere through massacres, persecution and sexual violence. In Nigeria and Colombia, Pentecostalism has enabled women to transform the domestic realm — to resist marital abuse, infidelity and male domination — with far-reaching social implications.[4] Similar stories are to be found within Judaism and Islam, and to some extent within Buddhism and Hinduism. Women's quest for religious liberation is not confined to liberals but spans the spectrum of belief from the profoundly orthodox to the radically innovative. Those working to reform their religions from within often do so in a spirit of critical cooperation with members of other denominations and faiths, so that ecumenism and inter-religious dialogue are accorded a high priority. While some of these women would describe themselves as feminists, others would feel ambivalent or even hostile towards feminism, although they might share many of its visions and goals.

This means that any brief analysis of the ways in which religion and gender intersect with regard to questions of social justice must be highly selective and simplified. The concepts of democracy, equality and human rights which inform many feminist arguments are rooted in a western world view with its Judaeo-Christian inheritance. Some argue that this makes all modern liberation movements, including feminism, inherently imperialistic and destructive of other cultures and religions.[5] This raises questions about the extent to which ideas of happiness and justice are culture-specific, so that what constitutes liberation in one culture might be experienced in another as a form of oppression. One might think of Muslim women who wear the veil to avoid being seen as sex objects in the highly sexualised public sphere of western culture, while westerners often interpret the veil as a sign of Islam's oppression of women.

These are complex issues and they do not lend themselves to easy solutions. That is why I have avoided the use of terms such as 'global sisterhood', which exaggerate the extent of international solidarity among women. I also sometimes refer to women theologians rather than feminist theologians to acknowledge that many non-western women maintain a critical distance from western feminism. I have tried to represent differences and disagreements fairly, to avoid creating a false impression of univocity or consensus. But after acknowledging all this, I would still argue that women today are experiencing a collective transformation in consciousness which cuts through historical boundaries, so that no society or institution is immune from its effects and many feel profoundly threatened by its consequences. Andrew Brown, writing in *The Spectator*, claims that 'The Catholic Church [...] is writhing in knots around feminism like a worm impaled on a hook.'[6]

In an article assessing the achievements of feminism, Nikki van der Gaag writes that 'Women still find themselves in impossible situations but because they are now more aware of their relative position in the world – and of the support they can get from other women – they are *reacting* differently.'[7] This change in reaction is often described as 'empowerment' and 'feminist consciousness'.

Empowerment refers to a process by which women individually and collectively realise their capacity to achieve change. It is a source of power arising from a sense of inner strength and self-worth, as opposed to a model of coercive power which depends on hierarchy, domination and control. The related idea of feminist consciousness sensitises people to the personal and social consequences of gender inequality. The idea of conscientisation is also found in liberation theology. It entails an acknowledgement that social ideologies which position groups in terms of class, race, gender or religion are as subtle as they are pervasive, so that they are not immediately obvious even to those whom they oppress or marginalise. When disadvantaged people become aware that their social positions are not divinely ordained or naturally ordered, but are the consequences of value systems and structures, they find the resources to challenge them and to pursue alternatives.

History will judge feminism and find it wanting in many ways. We cannot adequately assess a movement when we stand in its midst. As more and more women and men find the courage to speak out from their own experience of gender roles and sexual identities, it becomes clear that these issues and their impact on society are infinitely complex. Some have pointed out that feminist theology has failed to take seriously enough women's capacity to sin, so that there is sometimes a tendency to portray women as the innocent victims of male tyranny.[8] Clearly women do share responsibility for the damage that human beings inflict on one another and on the rest of creation. Wealthy western women are among the beneficiaries of the present economic order, and there is no evidence that women voters in the western democracies show any tendency to be more concerned than men with issues of social and economic justice. Feminist liberationist movements exclude many women and include many men. But feminism itself is proving to be a moment of crisis and change in the Christian tradition. Whatever legacy feminism leaves, post-feminist Christianity will not be the same as pre-feminist Christianity.

It is against this tapestry of light and dark, success and failure, fragile beginnings and sometimes brutal endings, that the arguments and visions of feminist theology have to be explored. While the intellectual task of feminist theology is concerned with the interpretation of Christian doctrine and symbolism, most feminist theologians are also actively involved with projects beyond the narrow domain of academic theology. The ethnographer Robin Nagle, in his study of liberation theology in Brazil, writes that 'Many people who today work to establish non-governmental organisations, to create political reform, to found women's health cooperatives, or to run for local and even state or federal offices had their start in base communities and in liberationist Catholicism.'[9] This suggests that politicised Christians often live out their social commitments in activities which are not explicitly identified as religious. In assessing the impact of Christian feminism, therefore, it is important not to concentrate only on church-led initiatives and explicitly Christian movements, but to consider wider contexts in which women are working collectively for change.

This *Comment* begins by identifying some of the issues of poverty and injustice that inform feminist liberation movements, and goes on to consider ways in which feminist consciousness influences women's experiences of Christianity both at the social and at the symbolic level. It offers a survey of women's theologies in various cultural contexts, to show how the shared concerns of feminism are shaped by the experiences of women in different situations. It then suggests ways in which core Christian symbols are being reinterpreted by women seeking to tell their stories of faith in ways which express their own deepest values, beliefs and hopes.

Christian feminism and social justice

The feminisation of poverty

A Kenyan friend, Esther Mombo, recently told me that 'feminism is saying no to what hurts'. To appreciate the task of feminism, one must first recognise what hurts women.

It is sometimes said that women are the poorest of the poor. The term 'the feminisation of poverty' refers to the fact women are likely to feel the effects of economic deprivation more acutely than men. Nearly two-thirds of all non-literate adults are women. Every year, more than half a million women die during pregnancy or childbirth, and more than 99 per cent of these deaths occur in developing countries. Research suggests a close link between education and reproductive health, with literate women tending to have fewer children.[10]

Domestic violence against women is a global problem. In Britain it is the second most common violent crime, accounting for more than 25 per cent of all violent crimes reported to the police. In Peru, wife-beating accounts for 70 per cent of crimes reported to police. In the United States, domestic violence is the leading cause of injury among women of reproductive age. In India, every day five women are burned in dowry-related disputes; women's groups claim the figure is closer to 25.[11]

Sexual and psychological violence against women is exacerbated by poverty and war. One young Somali Muslim woman, now working as a prostitute in Nairobi, describes how as a circumcised virgin she was taken hostage by gangsters, cut open with a razor and gang raped during the war in Somalia in the early 1990s. She fell pregnant and was ostracised by her religious community because she was regarded as defiled. To her relief her baby died at birth, but she still lives with a deep sense of shame. A Kenyan special correspondent writes that her story 'is not new or isolated. In the raging multi-dimensional factional war and the attendant hunger that have virtually consumed the former Italian colony, rape, battering of women and mutilation of their genitals is a part of the assault weapon in war.'[12] Another

African journalist, Ferial Haffajee, writes: 'When women from war zones tell their stories, there is no machismo but only stark reminders of the physical and mental devastation that conflicts bring. Women do not talk about the size and power of their guns, but of the magnitude and sadness of their losses.'[13]

Feminist theology does not claim academic or political neutrality. It acts and speaks in women's struggles for justice, working alongside other secular and religious campaigners who seek to combat the combined forces of economic and sexual exploitation, militarism, domestic violence and environmental abuse. Any form of liberation theology, including feminist liberation theology, recognises that the Christian promise of salvation does not apply only to life after death. It must be given concrete expression in the structures, politics and values of this world.

Signs of promise

While a great deal remains to be achieved in terms of justice for women, much has already been accomplished. Women's average life expectancy has improved in developing as well as developed countries and the percentage of women with no formal education has more than halved in one generation. Women almost everywhere are having fewer children and marrying later. In Brazil, the average number of births per woman has fallen from 6.1 in 1963 to 2.9 in 1993. Although women are still under-represented in politics, half the women elected heads of state or government in the twentieth century have come to power since 1990.[14]

In the past decade violence against women has been recognised as a gender issue, with the UN General Assembly proclaiming a Declaration on the Elimination of Violence Against Women in December 1993. In 1999, the Catholic Council of European Bishops' Conferences and the Conference of European Churches issued a joint letter on violence against women, in which they acknowledge that 'the churches have been silent for too long' and call for more open discussion about 'the attitudes and structures which nurture this violence.'[15]

All these developments provide grounds for cautious optimism, because they suggest that women's campaigns for greater representation do bear fruit. However, factors such as AIDS, the debt crisis, regional conflicts particularly in Africa and Eastern Europe, and the growing gulf between rich and poor could obliterate these hopeful beginnings. Although vast gender inequalities persist in all areas of public life, some believe that the feminist movement has outlived its relevance. There has been a powerful religious backlash against the women's movement, with groups of Roman Catholics, Protestant evangelicals and Muslims forming improbable alliances designed to force women back into domesticity and out of public life. So, after nearly three decades of a global women's movement, there is a little to celebrate and a great deal still to be done.

Gender, the United Nations and the Vatican

In the past decade, the United Nations (UN) has staged a number of conferences aimed at raising the international profile of women's rights and gender issues. The Fourth World Conference on Women, in Beijing in September 1995, produced a platform for action which 189 countries signed. In June 2000, a Beijing Plus Five conference was held at the UN headquarters, coinciding with the launch of a new biennial report, *Progress of the World's Women 2000*.

However, some women express disquiet about the ways in which western feminist concerns dominate the UN agenda, leaving little space for discussion of fundamental issues of violence and economic oppression in the Third World. According to one Zambian delegate, Gladys Mutukwa, African NGOs at Beijing Plus Five were 'made to feel like intruders on the process'.[16] A Kenyan newspaper which refers to the conference as Beijing Minus Five reports that 'A cursory glance at the draft outcome document shows that no ground has been won on the critical gender concerns highlighted as vital for African women.'[17] This failure by the United Nations to offer an effective platform for African women is even more disturbing in the light of a recent survey which shows that the gap between Africa and the industrialised world has widened over the last 30 years. The average gross national product (GNP) of African countries is now only 7 per cent of that for industrialised countries.[18]

The Vatican, uniquely among the world's religious institutions, has Non-Member State Permanent Observer status in the UN General Assembly. In the past, the Holy See has used its influence to champion human rights, but as reproductive health and family planning have come to the fore it has become a dissenting voice. At the International Conference on Population and Development (ICPD) in Cairo in 1994, Vatican delegates joined forces with some Islamic states to block some resolutions and modify others. Since then the Holy See has intensified its campaign against the UN commitment to population control.

As a result, an international campaign was launched in 1999 by a coalition of religious groups, women's groups and other NGOs, calling for an official review of the Vatican's status at the United Nations. The campaign is actively promoted by the pressure group, Catholics for a Free Choice (CFFC). The main areas of concern are the resistance of the Catholic hierarchy to the use of condoms to prevent the spread of HIV/AIDS, its absolute opposition to abortion even in cases of rape, and its condemnation of all artificial methods of birth control. Bene Madunagu, executive board chair of the Girls' Power Initiative in Nigeria, claims that the Vatican's interventions and lobbying in the United Nations 'deny women in developing countries access to protection that Catholic women in the developed world enjoy, as they have the economic and social power to ignore the pronouncements of the church hierarchy'.[19]

However, without denying the seriousness of these charges, there are other issues at stake. The Holy See's delegation to Beijing was led by Professor Mary Ann Glendon, a Harvard law professor who once worked for the black civil rights movement in Mississippi. The team included Kathryn Hawa Hoomkwap, a former Nigerian health minister and mother of four who was imprisoned for nine months during a military takeover. Annabel Miller, reporting on the Beijing conference in *The Tablet*, writes that these women 'had clearly been chosen not only for their loyalty to the Church, but for their intellectual – and street – credibility'. She goes on to say that 'this was not enough to break through the wall of prejudice, even hatred, among some secular feminists.'[20]

In Glendon's summary remarks on the conference, she points to a 'close correspondence' between Catholic social teaching and what she calls 'the living heart' of the Beijing documents which focus on 'the needs of women in poverty, on strategies for development, on literacy and education, on ending violence against women, on a culture of peace, and on access to employment, land and capital, and technology'. Yet she goes on to express regret over the 'exaggerated individualism' which leads the text to neglect issues such as the importance of motherhood, and to pay disproportionate attention to sexual reproductive health. She writes, 'A document that respects women's dignity should address the health of the whole woman. A document that respects women's intelligence should devote at least as much attention to literacy as to fertility.'[21]

If UN women's conferences are indeed being hijacked by the concerns of the affluent nations, then it would seem imperative that the Catholic Church is encouraged to use its influence to ensure that all women are fairly represented. Patricia Stoat, a British feminist Catholic, writes, 'Just because the Holy See doesn't have a constituency to please it can – or could – be a prophetic voice in the counsels of the UN where pragmatism and wheeler-dealing would otherwise go unchallenged'.[22] The Christian belief in the absolute value of the person and the imperative to encompass all aspects of human life within the concept of justice can offer a voice of critical resistance to international policies which are driven primarily by economic concerns. Given the powerful role of the western democracies in the United Nations, it might be naïve to believe that the Vatican is an obstructive voice in what would otherwise be a democratic and egalitarian institution. While the church's teaching on birth control is widely rejected among Catholics, that does not mean that the 'contraceptive mentality' of modern western society is a solution. The Ghanaian feminist theologian, Mercy Amba Oduyoye, criticises the 'anti-baby economy of the North' which is being foisted on the South. She writes:

> Mothering is a religious duty. It is what a good socio-political and economic system should be about if the human beings entrusted to the state are to be fully human. [. . .] Scarcely ever does one find a deliberate choice of childlessness among African women and furthest from our understanding of life is to make that choice for economic reasons.[23]

The Vatican's role *vis à vis* the United Nations highlights some of the questions which surround the relationship between religious values and women's rights in the modern world. On the one hand, male religious hierarchies can prove powerful obstacles to women's struggles for greater self-determination and freedom of choice, particularly over fertility and reproduction. On the other hand, religious values can provide a critique of the rampant materialism and individualism of modern society, and afford women a platform from which to explore alternative possibilities beyond the control of global economic and political institutions.

Women's theologies in context

Feminism and the Catholic church

Catholic feminist theology emerged in the aftermath of the Second Vatican Council in the late 1960s and 1970s. It was inspired by a combination of the new theological freedom afforded to women in the church after the Council, and by the emergence of the women's movement in the western democracies. Vatican II continues to generate debate among Catholics about a variety of issues, including the role of women in the church, and both conservative and liberal theologians have written extensively about the influence of feminism on Christianity. Pope John Paul II has called for

> a 'new feminism' which rejects the temptation of imitating models of 'male domination', in order to acknowledge and affirm the true genius of women in every aspect of the life of society, and overcome all discrimination, violence and exploitation.[24]

Feminism questions many traditional Christian beliefs about human nature, sexuality and God, in a way which has ramifications for ethics, social justice, family life and personal relationships, and for the language of doctrine and worship. For some, such as William Oddie, editor of the *Catholic Herald*, it threatens the future of Christianity.[25] For others, it announces the dawn of a new age as the church at last begins to give full expression to the message of Galatians 3:

> All baptised in Christ, you have all clothed yourselves in Christ, and there are no more distinctions between Jew and Greek, slave and free, male and female, but all of you are one in Christ Jesus. (Gal.3:27-28)

The emergence of feminist theology has stimulated a discussion among women in the world's religious traditions, who recognise that it was initially too focused on the concerns of white, middle-class women and did not adequately represent the perspectives of Third World women and women of colour. There are now feminist movements in virtually all the world's major religions and cultures. The Indian feminist, Urvashi Butalia, describing the growing diversity within the women's movement, writes:

> as we look back on a century of women's activism, this recognition of difference, this understanding of its infinite variety, this turning of the gaze from the North to the South and back again, is perhaps the most valuable contribution of the women's movement the world over.[26]

What is feminist theology?

The critical principle of feminist theology is the promotion of the full humanity of women. Whatever denies, diminishes, or distorts the full humanity of women is, therefore, appraised as not redemptive. Theologically speaking, whatever diminishes or denies the full humanity of women must be presumed not to reflect the divine or an authentic relation to the divine, or to reflect the authentic nature of things, or to be the message or work of an authentic redeemer or a community of redemption.

This negative principle also implies the positive principle: what does promote the full humanity of women is of the Holy, it does reflect true relation to the divine, it is the true nature of things, the authentic message of redemption and the mission of redemptive community.

From: Rosemary Radford Ruether, *Sexism and God-Talk – Towards a Feminist Theology*, SCM, London, 1992, pp18-19.

Rosemary Radford Ruether's definition (see above) has found widespread acceptance within Christian feminism, and it forms one of its basic premises. Its theological method takes women's experience as its starting point, recognising that until now theology has been done exclusively by men and is therefore based on men's experience of self, God and the world. The exclusion and silencing of women means that theology has developed as a one-sided form of knowledge, and the appeal to women's experience helps to correct this masculine bias.

The full humanity of women refers not to a fixed principle but to a way of being open in faith to all that is life-giving and liberating in terms of women's potential, and of recognising and rejecting what distorts or destroys that potential. It is a commitment to spiritual and social change which is aware of the boundaries of knowledge, not only in terms of each individual but also in terms of each cultural, historical and gendered point of view. It seeks wisdom and understanding through women's experiences of joy and suffering, hope and despair, across cultural, ethnic and geographical boundaries, in recognition of the fact that learning how to be fully human is a way of life and not a theoretical position.

Feminist theology and women's theologies

In acknowledging that the term 'full humanity' encompasses a range of experiences and insights, feminist theology commits itself to accommodating different voices. Many women's theologies have flourished in engagement with feminism, but not necessarily in sympathy with all the arguments of white western feminists. To express both a relationship to and a distance from western feminism, these diverse theologies use a variety of names to describe themselves. They include, among others, womanist theology (arising out of the experiences of Black North American women), *dalit* women's theology (which explores the situation of low caste Christian women in India), concerned African women's theology (primarily focusing on the encounter between African culture, Christianity and feminism), *minjung* feminist theology (Korean women's theology from the perspective of the poor and the marginalised), and *mujerista* theology (informed by the experiences of Hispanic American women).[27]

Women's theologies are often descriptive rather than analytic, and those looking for systematic argument are likely to be disappointed. Where women's experience refuses to conform to the priorities of academic theology, feminist theology tends to set aside the latter to give space to the former. Theological language yields to a more poetic idiom informed by literature, folklore, art, music and the everyday metaphors and images of women's lives as mothers, lovers, wives, sisters, friends and seekers after God. The Brazilian theologian, Ivone Gebara, writes,

When women's experience is expressed in a church whose tradition is machistic, the other side of human experience returns to theological discourse: the side of the person who gives birth, nurses, nourishes, of the person who for centuries has remained silent with regard to anything having to do with theology. Now she begins to express her experience of God, in another manner, a manner that does not demand that reason alone be regarded as the single and universal mediation of theological discourse.[28]

Accommodating difference

How far is it possible to accommodate diversity, without succumbing to relativism? Does feminist theology risk privileging so many voices that in the end its original vision becomes lost in a cacophony of competing perspectives? Some might say that the wording of this question betrays a masculine way of thinking, following a form of rationality which values unity over plurality, conformity over diversity, identity over difference. Many feminists argue the need for alternative modes of reasoning, in which harmony, plurality and equality are the guiding principles, rather than uniformity, singularity and hierarchy. The image of the web is often used to suggest a pattern of thought different from the linear logic of the western intellectual tradition.

But feminist liberation theology might also be able to sustain a commitment to plurality because it finds its common ground in social ethics rather than doctrine. All the theologies surveyed here share a commitment to 'the preferential option for the poor' and to identifying the ways in which being a woman is in itself a cause of economic and cultural impoverishment in a world dominated by masculine values. Feminist theology's commitment to plurality entails a concern for the well-being of women which is equally concerned for the well-being of men, for neither sex can flourish in the shadow of the other's oppression. It is a vision which is implicitly or explicitly informed by the belief that all human beings whatever their sex, race, creed, age or ability are equally made in the image of God.

This means speaking out against a world order in which poverty, deprivation and exploitation are built into the fabric of global politics and economics; a world in which we invest more in arms than in education, health care and social welfare; a world in which the poor labour under miserable conditions to sustain the lifestyles and increase the profits of the rich; a world in which women and children are commodified in a burgeoning sex industry. There is nothing necessary or essential about this

17

way of organising human relationships. The world order is a human construct which humans can transform.

A world-wide vision

The World Council of Churches (WCC) and the Ecumenical Association of Third World Theologians (EATWOT) have provided an international forum for the development of women's theologies. Formed in Tanzania in 1976, EATWOT initially provided a meeting point for theologians from Africa, Asia and Latin America, and later also for minority groups in the United States and Europe. The feminist theologian Ursula King identifies EATWOT's unifying concerns as:

> a stress on liberation as the central core of the Christian gospel, the need to reread the Bible in the light of the hermeneutical privilege of the poor, and a rejection of the dominant theologies of Europe and the USA.[29]

This emergence of a collective theological voice from the underside has been described as an 'irruption of the Third World into theology'.[30] However, at the 1981 meeting of EATWOT in New Delhi, women spoke out vigorously against their exclusion from EATWOT discussions, initiating what has been described as 'the irruption within the irruption'.[31] Since then, nearly 20 years of women's theological activity has given rise to a world-wide movement of reflection and social action, inspired by the principles of feminism and liberation theology, but seeking distinctive forms of expression and practice which are appropriate to the cultural contexts in which women find themselves. It is impossible to include all these different theological voices here, but the following selection gives a sense of the commonality and the diversity of women's theologies.

Latin American feminist theology

For many Latin American women politicised during the liberation struggles of the 1970s and 1980s, feminism introduced a new gendered perspective to their understanding of justice. They began to recognise that the political involvement which accompanied liberation theology often increased their workload and their subservience to men's agendas. Nagle writes that during

Planned to operate in three stages, the women's project sought:

To broaden our understanding of women's situation in our respective socio-economic, political, and religio-cultural realities.

To discover the vital aspects of women's experience of God in emerging spiritualities.

To reread the Bible from Third World women's perspective in the light of total liberation.

To articulate faith reflections on women's realities, struggles, and spirituality.

To deepen our commitment and solidarity to work toward full humanity for all.

Spiritual experience for women of the Third World thus means being in communion with all those who fight for life. This is our motivation for doing theology, which is done with the body, the heart, the mind, the total self – all penetrated by the Holy Spirit.

Compassion and solidarity are main elements of this spirituality and this theology, and this is expressed in action: organised, patient and loving action.[32]

Extract from the Final Document of the Intercontinental Women's Conference sponsored by EATWOT and held at Oaxtepec, Mexico on December 6, 1986.

his study of liberation theology in northern Brazil, he met many nuns who 'felt that they had been doing the community-level work essential to liberationism for many years, but that it only received attention when the Boff brothers – monk Clodovis and priest Leonardo – "discovered" it and made it the focus of their writings'.[33]

Pamela Hussey and Marigold Best interviewed 30 women in El Salvador in 1994, including feminist activists, religious sisters and villagers. Time and again, the women describe ways in which liberation theology and feminism together have given them new courage and commitment in their struggle for justice. Hussey and Best acknowledge that the women they interviewed 'represent only a conscientised minority in El Salvador',[34] but they point to the importance of what one woman called 'a growing "spirituality of resistance" to the dominant ideology which tries to persuade us all that there is no alternative'.[35]

Liberation theology became a project of the poor but it did not wake us up as women because we were just part of 'the people'. We took on responsibilities without becoming aware that we had three full-time jobs to do: work outside the home, housework, and our commitment as activists. We did not see that. We were so tired. We couldn't take part in the executive council because we didn't know how to read or write. But we did not understand why.

It was the feminist movement that shook us up as women because it helped us to ask questions. [...] Feminist theology gave a 90 degree turn to our lives and actions. A personal challenge for me is to be part of the movement of the popular church, starting with awareness of gender conditioning, and questioning how power is used in the Christian base communities.

Isabel Ascencio, quoted in Marigold Best and Pamela Hussey, *Life out of Death: The feminine spirit in El Salvador*, CIIR, London, 1996, p150.

The Marxist economic critique which informed early liberation theology was inadequate to address the many forms of oppression perpetuated not only through class systems but also through racial and sexual inequalities, for example. Today, the political insights of liberation theology are being integrated into a broader framework informed by women's experiences of exploitation in a society which is still governed by the values of machismo. Sometimes, this requires a transformed theological vision rather than a modification of earlier models. For example, the Brazilian feminist Ivone Gebara has questioned the fundamental premises of liberation theology, arguing that it is driven by the same patriarchal values which informed earlier theologies. She writes:

I confess that the image of God as liberator presents problems for me and also for the impoverished, who are always the first victims even of just struggles for political, economic, and cultural liberation. We arrive at the paradox of dying and of 'living' in a state of mortal armed aggression in the name of the God of life. [...]

> In practice this image of God as liberator excludes women as much as does the image of God as 'the Other,' insofar as women continue to be the pietás of war games, accepting on their knees the murdered bodies of husbands, lovers, brothers, sisters, children, parents [...] [36]

Latin American feminist theologians, like their counterparts in other parts of the world, resist sexual violence against women, while reclaiming a more positive and life-affirming attitude towards female sexuality than that offered by traditional Christianity. A Colombian theologion Ana María Bidegain in a survey of the impact of Christianity on Latin America, describes the ways in which a preoccupation with the sinfulness of sex led Christians to focus on this to the exclusion of more important issues of politics and justice. She sees one of the tasks of Latin American men and women as being not only to work for a more just political order, but also to call for 'the actualisation of a dimension that has always existed in Christianity [...] It is God who created humanity sexed. Sexuality is a gift of God.' [37]

There has been a powerful backlash against Latin American liberation theology, not only from the Vatican but also from new evangelical and pentecostal churches which have gained considerable influence. But like their theological predecessors, Latin American women work within a relatively homogeneous religious and cultural environment. Catholicism tends to be the main source of their theological symbols and doctrines, although there is a growing recognition that indigenous cultures offer rich resources for the recovery of forgotten spiritual traditions. Women's theologies in other parts of the world reveal a more pluralistic picture.

Asian women's theologies

Asian theologians work in a context of religious plurality and one where, with the exception of the Philippines and East Timor, Christianity is a minority religion. The Korean poet and feminist theologian, Sun Ai Lee-Park, identifies 'religious-cultural alienation' [38] as a key factor in Asian women's lives. Women form alliances across religious boundaries, working together to challenge sexism and inter-religious conflict and to harness the spiritual energy and liberating potential inherent in Asia's religious traditions. There is a variety of Asian women's theologies, which reflect regional and religious differences while seeking to establish harmonious interaction between the religions.

The journal, *In God's Image* (*IGI*), was started in 1982 by Sun Ai, as a forum for theological discussion among Asian women. When she died in 1999, one of the tributes noted her willingness to address topics that were taboo in most church circles. 'Going through the back issues of *IGI* we find articles on abortion, prostitution, violence against women side by side with poems, bible studies and liturgies that bind these issues together with the beauty of creation and the loving, just God.'[39] This suggests something of the diversity of issues which inform Asian women's theology, and the spirituality which unites them in a vision of a renewed creation.

Poor Asian women suffer acutely as a result of the environmental crisis, from the floods in Bangladesh to the forest fires in Indonesia and Malaysia. One woman writing in the aftermath of the fires says that 'the image of Asia now is of dark, gloomy and smoky haze, of collapse, chaos and crisis. Globalisation has revealed its capricious and cruel side.'[40] Concern for the environment is a powerful motivating force for Asian feminist scholars and activists to work together, critically analysing the ways in which patriarchal values and the global economy militate against environmental and human well-being, while also seeking to recover some of the holistic attitudes towards nature found in traditional Asian spiritualities.

In many parts of Asia, particularly those affected by tourism or having a significant American military presence, the sex industry presents a growing problem. Although exact figures are difficult to obtain, a 1997 study assessed the number of child prostitutes in the Philippines to be about 75,000, and in Thailand a 1993 survey suggested that between 30,000 and 35,000 children were involved in prostitution.[41] Marianne Katoppo, an Indonesian theologian, writes: 'The present secular society is one in which practically everything has been transformed into commodities, including human relationships. Sex, as one of the most intensive forms of relationships, has turned into a prime commodity.'[42] In the Philippines, the Benedictine sister and theologian, Mary John Mananzan, is a founder member of GABRIELA, a coalition of 105 women's organisations which recently launched an international initiative known as the Purple Rose campaign, described in the publicity material as 'a massive global campaign to expose and fight sex trafficking and its perpetrators'.[43]

Liberation theology in India has taken a distinctive form known as *dalit* theology, the *dalits* being those formerly known as 'untouchables' in the

Hindu caste system. One report describes the church in India as 'a *dalit* church', because 70 per cent of India's 25 million Christians (mostly Catholics) are *dalits*.[44] A paper issued in December 1999 describes *dalit* women as '*dalits* within *dalits*', arguing that 'the intersection of caste and gender means that they are subject to the most extreme forms of violence, discrimination and exploitation, even at the hands of women from upper-castes.'[45] The literacy rate for *dalit* women is less than 24 per cent, which is about half the level of that of non-*dalit* women. Almost 90 per cent of *dalit* women work outside the home, mostly in the informal sector, but their pay is less than half of that earned by their male counterparts. The report argues that it is necessary to address *dalit* women's concerns as distinct from those of upper-caste women and of *dalit* men. *Dalit* theology is still in its infancy, but already women theologians are seeking to express a gendered vision of liberation based on *dalit* women's experiences of suffering, faith and hope.

I saw at least 400 Christian *dalit* women, each with a heavy headload of a bag (with utensils and clothes) and two or three children with each of them, rushing to get into the train along with their men. They prayed before they boarded the train, as a group, as a community. They were migrating to other places for agricultural work, leaving their homes and hearths. In the new places they have to live under trees or in open places or sometimes in the cattle sheds. During this period they virtually live under the pleasure and the will of the landlords and the middlemen. They will continue to pray and sing and struggle. This scene reminded that I was going to Madras to talk about these very women and to formulate theology for them, and I began to laugh at myself. I was reminded about their Christian faith. They are the ones who are the givers to the Church. They are the ones who are the cross-bearers of the congregation. They are the ones who are the torch-bearers of the faith. They practice *dalit* theology in their day-to-day life, whereas we are struggling to formulate *dalit* theology. What a contrast it [46]

Swarnatha Devi, a woman theologian speaking at a conference of the Christian Dalit Liberation Movement, describing *dalit* women waiting to board a train in the Indian region of Andhra Pradesh.

Among the predominantly Protestant Christians of South Korea, *minjung* theology draws on a rich blend of eastern and western traditions to inform its vision of liberation. Traditionally '*minjung*' means the socially downtrodden and excluded, and the word is now associated with the struggle for democracy and human rights among South Korean Christians. The Korea Association of Christian Women for Women *Minjung* (KACWWM) was founded in 1986 as an ecumenical group committed to offering practical and political support to *minjung* women. As well as providing nursery schools and fighting for fair working conditions, KACWWM campaigns for arms reduction, peace and national reunification, and for grassroot democracy projects.

Women *minjung* theologians incorporate aspects of Shamanism into their theology, recognising that women are the main practitioners of this form of religion. The feminist *minjung* theologian, Chung Hyun Kyung, says of herself that 'my bowel is Shamanist, my heart is Buddhist and my head is Christian'.[47] This suggests how Asian women's religious identities are formed out of a rich syncretistic vision, which can be threatening to western Christian beliefs. Kyung provoked controversy when she performed a ritual invocation of the *han*-ridden spirits at the plenary session of the Seventh Assembly of the WCC in Canberra in 1991 (see box opposite). Han refers to the grief and resentment of those who have been killed unjustly, but which can be transformed into the raw energy required for liberation and transformation.

Kyung refers to the need for 'survival-liberation centered syncretism'.[49] She asks, 'What makes Christianity Christian? How far can we make ourselves vulnerable in order to be both truly Asian and truly Christian?'[50] The answer to this question will emerge gradually as a distinctively Asian form of Christianity takes shape. It is impossible to predict what the contours of such a Christianity might be, or how women might find in Asian spirituality a resource for the recovery of the feminine dimension of God which has been eclipsed in the western church. But if at the end of the second millennium Christianity traces its development through the ideas of Plato and Aristotle and the pagan festivals of the ancient European world, it seems just as likely that by the end of the third millennium that list will include the rich religious heritage of Asia.

Women and Christianity in Africa

Turning from Asia to Africa, the basic issues of poverty, exploitation and environmental degradation remain the same, but Africa also poses distinctive

Come. The spirit of Hagar, Egyptian, black slave woman exploited and abandoned by Abraham and Sarah, the ancestors of our faith (Gen. 21.15-21).

Come. The spirit of male babies killed by the soldiers of king Herod upon Jesus' birth.

Come. The spirit of Joan of Arc, and of the many other women burnt at the 'witch trials' throughout the medieval era.

Come. The spirit of the people who died during the Crusades.

Come. The spirit of Jewish people killed in the gas chambers during the holocaust.

Come. The spirit of people killed in Hiroshima and Nagasaki by atomic bombs.

Come. The spirit of Korean women in the Japanese 'prostitution army' during World War II, used and torn by violence-hungry soldiers.

Come. The spirit of Vietnamese people killed by napalm, Agent Orange, or hunger on the drifting boats.

Come. The spirit of earth, air and water, raped, tortured and exploited by human greed for money.

Come. The spirit of the Liberator, our brother Jesus, tortured and killed on the cross.[48]

Extract from Chung Hyun Kyung's Plenary Address to the Seventh Assembly of the World Council of Churches in Canberra, Australia, in February 1991.

challenges to Christianity today. Some writers have referred to Africa as 'anthropologically impoverished.'[51] Not only does the continent suffer economically but its cultural heritage has been undermined by colonialism and the slave trade. Africa was colonised by many powers and the continent has no common language or religion. Islam and Christianity are often locked in violent conflict. In countries which formed part of the British empire, Protestant Christianity is the norm, whereas in former French and Portuguese colonies, Catholicism is more widespread. Whereas in French- and English-speaking Africa theologians between the 1950s and 1980s tended to focus on inculturation, in apartheid South Africa a political or contextual theology emerged. This was at first influenced by the Black Consciousness movement and therefore had more in common with North American Black theology, but later took on a distinctive form. However, with the end of apartheid theological concerns have converged, so that both inculturation and liberation now feature prominently on the African theological agenda.

Perhaps the greatest threat to sub-Saharan Africa now is the AIDS pandemic. A UN report published in June 2000 estimated that more than one-third of today's 15-year-olds will die of AIDS in the worst-affected countries. The report also estimates that the prevalence of HIV in women aged 15-24 is two or three times higher than among young men. This is because 'Girls who consent or are coerced into early intercourse are especially vulnerable to infection, not only because of their immature genital tract but because they often have older partners, who are more likely to be infected.'[52] Traditional healers sometimes advise men with AIDS to have sex with young virgins as a cure for the disease. AIDS can also have a devastating impact on family life, with poor grandparents left to care for orphaned children who might themselves have been infected through their mothers. But the UN report points out that African governments are paying four times more in debt service than they spend on health and education.

Poverty divides African women from their western feminist counterparts and allies them closely with men in their own culture. For this reason, African women theologians choose to describe themselves as 'Concerned African Women Theologians' rather than as feminist theologians, because the latter implies too close a conformity to the priorities and values of western feminism. When one's children are starving and structural adjustment policies are destroying the fabric of society, anxieties about professional glass ceilings and the right to sexual self-expression can seem far removed from reality.

Religion has a widespread influence in African cultures where the spirit world is experienced as a potent factor in nature and everyday life. The debate between men and women theologians has focused sharply on inculturation and the position of women in traditional religions as well as in Christianity and Islam. As in Latin America, when theologically educated women began to consider the claims and arguments of male theologians, they found them lacking in gender-awareness and perpetuating traditional religious practices which oppressed women. The Nigerian theologian, Daisy Nwachuku, asks:

> If liberation and freedom culminating in the worshiper's ultimate salvation is a basic theological concept, should the African woman who first observed the traditional religion but later chose Christianity, be forced retrogressively into bondage she renounced? [...] Within the context of liberation theology, one might ask whether cultural inhumanity in the form of religious sexism, prejudices, stigmatization, and stereotyping should be enthroned when the white racism that sought to suppress African culture is dethroned.[53]

African Christian women are engaged in a complex task of cultural reclamation and transformation, identifying those aspects of traditional belief and practice which enrich their Christian faith, and those which are oppressive and should not be incorporated into Christianity in the name of inculturation. For example, some argue that while the outlawing of polygamy can create serious social problems for wives who find themselves abandoned and left to care for themselves and their children, women rarely see polygamy as a desirable form of marriage. Widowhood rites are usually more demanding for women than for men and can mean prolonged periods of extreme mourning. The Ghanaian government introduced an Act of Widowhood Rites to prevent some of the abuses suffered by widowed women in the name of traditional practices, but the Ghanaian theologian Elizabeth Amoah questions the impact of such legislation on the lives of illiterate women in rural areas.[54]

On the positive side, African women argue that some traditional rituals associated with, for example, childbearing and menstruation, can be reinterpreted within the church to express and celebrate aspects of women's lives which have been excluded from western Christianity. In addition, independent churches are proliferating across Africa, and these spirit-led movements often allow women significant roles as prophets and healers.

Traditional religions are also beginning to play a significant role in environmental campaigns in some parts of Africa, with environmentalists recognising that there can be a fruitful interaction between protection of the environment and preservation of sacred places. A Zimbabwean sociologist, Sara C. Mvududu, has shown how women spirit mediums can encourage women to rediscover and respect traditional ways of managing woodlands, bearing in mind that poor rural women are largely responsible for agriculture. The Association of Zimbabwe Traditional Environmental Conservation (AZTREC) has 14 women's groups establishing nurseries and tree-planting programmes, with spirit mediums providing an important educational function in establishing sacred areas for conservation.[55]

The main concerns of African women theologians can be summarised as first, sustaining a Christian critique against an economic order which has inflicted widespread poverty on the continent; and second, contributing to a distinctively African form of Christianity which incorporates the best aspects of traditional values and practices, while using Gospel values to challenge those which are oppressive or unjust towards women.

Womanist theology

Black American women have given rise to a new theological vision which has had a widespread influence on feminist theology. The term 'womanist' comes from the expression 'womanish' which is described as 'Usually referring to outrageous, audacious, courageous or willful behavior. Wanting to know more and in greater depth than is considered "good" for one.'[56] Alice Walker writes that 'Womanist is to feminist as purple to lavender.'[57]

Womanist theology is primarily a North American Protestant movement which developed in critical engagement with black theology – a form of liberation theology developed by black American Christians such as James Cone since the 1970s. Like other contextual feminist theologies, it arises from a recognition that men's theological visions often fail to take gender into account, and therefore fail to recognise how women can be doubly oppressed: black women suffer alongside black men as victims of racism, but they also suffer at the hands of black men as victims of sexism. In addition, the experience of slavery gives black Americans a very different perspective on American history and culture from that of white Americans, and requires a different Christian narrative from that which was used to justify slavery and colonialism. When black Americans read the scriptures, they discovered a message of liberation and hope in the midst of enslavement, poverty and historical alienation.

Womanists place a strong emphasis on the reclamation of black women's sense of self-worth and on the need to affirm their sexuality, given generations of sexual humiliation and abuse by both white and black men.

Delores Williams argues that the experience of sexual abuse under slavery robbed women of the language of the erotic. Womanist writers such as bell hooks and Alice Walker seek to create positive images which liberate black women's sexuality from the negative associations built around it by white culture and slavery. This is encompassed in a broader celebration of nature, divinity and community, expressed in Walker's description of a womanist as someone who 'Loves music. Loves dance. Loves the moon. Loves the Spirit. Loves love and food and roundness. Loves struggle. *Loves* the Folk. Loves herself. *Regardless*.'[58]

The art of story-telling features highly in womanist thought. Black mothers have always told stories of wisdom and survival to their daughters. Women such as Harriet Tubman, known as the Moses of her people because of her work in liberating slaves, and Sojourner Truth, a freed slave and popular preacher, are celebrated as heroines and role models for black women seeking to reclaim their histories and identities. Black writers and poets such as Toni Morrison, Alice Walker and Audré Lorde offer an alternative language and vision for those excluded from the values and ethics of white Americans. The womanist ethicist, Katie Geneva Cannon, writing of the importance of women's literature for forming new ethical paradigms, says:

> The cherished ethical ideas predicated upon the existence of freedom and a wide range of choices proved null and void in situations of oppression. The real-lived texture of Black life requires moral agency that may run contrary to the ethical boundaries of mainline Protestantism.[59]

Conclusion

This *Comment* can offer only a fleeting glimpse of the kaleidoscopic vision of women's theologies. The picture is constantly changing as more and more voices emerge from the silence of women's history. I have not discussed the theological perspectives of Australian aboriginal women, Hispanic women's liberation theology (*mujerista* theology), the theology of Christian Palestinian women, nor women's theologies from other faiths. All these reveal different facets of the ways in which liberation, faith and women's rights encounter one another in the contemporary world, and each would be worthy of a study in its own right.

Reinterpreting the Christian tradition

Feminist theologians recognise that theological symbols and social structures are interdependent. When people become aware of a discontinuity between their lived experiences of faith and the language of doctrine, theology and ethics, there is a need for a mutual process of transformation. Just as the Christian narrative has the power to challenge and inspire patterns of behaviour and lifestyle, so the lives of those within the Christian tradition have the power to challenge and inspire the narrative. Thus any living faith tradition grows and evolves in creative interaction with the lives of its adherents.

God, Christ and the Spirit

Feminists argue that there is a close relationship between concepts of God and the social order, so that theology both influences and is influenced by the structures and values of society. Because Christian concepts of God are shaped by masculine projections and patriarchal social values, Christianity has tended to reinforce the patriarchal status quo. A central task of feminist theology is to explore new ways of speaking about God which challenge the use of exclusively masculine and paternal images and metaphors.

Christianity has always taught that ultimately God is mystery beyond all naming and beyond any human attributes, including gender. God is neither male nor female, and both male and female human beings are equally like and unlike God. So when feminists attribute feminine characteristics and maternal qualities to God they are not claiming to define or describe God but are rather naming God differently, in order to create a more inclusive form of theological language. This offers women a language of faith which allows them to relate to God in terms of their own gender and life experience. It also exposes the contradiction between the claim that God is beyond gender and the insistence that God can be referred to only in the language of fatherhood and masculinity.

From a feminist liberationist perspective, Christian ideas about God depend too heavily on images of power, conquest and domination, which reflect the values of an imperialist church intent on conquering the world. The writings of African and Asian women, in particular, seek emancipating images which are not associated with western colonialism. The Kenyan theologian, Teresa M. Hinga, outlines the destructive consequences of the missionaries' representation of Jesus as 'the warrior King, in whose name and banner (the cross), new territories, both physical and spiritual, would be fought for, annexed and subjugated. An imperial Christianity [...] had an imperial Christ to match.'[60] She identifies three alternative images which African women use to express their faith: Jesus Christ as personal friend and saviour who meets women at the point of their greatest need; Christ as the embodiment of the spirit, particularly in the independent churches in which a 'pneumatic christology' allows Christ to become 'the voice of the voiceless, the power of the powerless'[61]; and third, Christ as the 'iconoclastic prophet' who 'stands out in Scripture as a critic of the status quo, particularly when it engenders social injustices and marginalization of some in society'.[62]

Such reinterpretations of Christ's identity reject images which seem to justify the oppression of women or to perpetuate violence. Mary John Mananzan writes:

> The most harmful image of God is that of God personified as male, a warrior, the Absolute Other up in heaven, a jealous God, a father who demanded the sacrifice of his only son in atonement for sins. This has been used to legitimise child abuse and to foster a victim attitude among women. The image of Jesus as sacrificed lamb has likewise induced women to follow the path of 'innocent victimhood'. There is a need to reconstruct the life-giving images which are fluid and dynamic, compassionate and liberating, cosmic and encompassing of all creation, space and time.[63]

Such arguments invite an alternative vision of the Christian life as one of fecundity, celebration and life, rather than sacrifice, denial and death. The Christian belief that God became human thus becomes a story not of punishment and sin but of the most radical possible affirmation of the human made in the image of God. Liberation theologians, including feminist liberationists, point out that in becoming human God also became a poor Jew born of a poor woman on the edges of the Roman empire. At the heart of Christianity, therefore, is an invitation to recognise God's special love for the poor, the marginalised and the oppressed. David Tombs recently added a controversial new perspective, arguing that Jesus' torture and crucifixion at the hands of the Romans would have included elements of sexual humiliation akin to that suffered by many victims of torture in Latin America.[64] Thus Jesus expresses the solidarity of God with the most abject and abused of all human beings.

The womanist theologian, Delores Williams, points out that images of Christ as the surrogate victim who suffers and dies on behalf of others are deeply problematic for black American women, whose history of slavery, servitude and sexual abuse has too often made them suffering surrogates for others. She writes:

> The surrogacy roles black women have filled during slavery and beyond [...] rob African-American women of self-consciousness, self-care, and self-esteem, and put them in the service of other people's desires tasks, and goals. [...] It is therefore altogether fitting and proper for black women to ask whether the image of a surrogate-God has salvific power for black women, or whether this image of redemption supports and reinforces the exploitation that has accompanied their experience with surrogacy. If black women accept this image of redemption, can they not also passively accept the exploitation surrogacy brings?[65]

Williams poses a dramatic challenge to many traditional Christian beliefs, and it remains to be seen how far the boundaries of the tradition can stretch to accommodate such challenges. Inevitably a tension exists between any attempt to redefine core Christian symbolism and the need to sustain the integrity and coherence of the Christian story. But for many women theologians that story will become more coherent when it is more inclusive. This is particularly true when it comes to feminist biblical interpretation.

The Bible

Feminists adopt methods of reading the Bible similar to those of liberation theologians. They recognise that all readings are subjective, and all interpretations of texts reflect to some extent the identities and values of their readers. Given that the Bible has been interpreted mainly by educated western men, its meanings have been understood in the social contexts to which these men belong. By assuming a different sexual, racial or cultural identity, a reader might discern new interpretations. To read the Bible as a black woman, for example, is to discover a different message in stories such as that of Hagar and the angel (Gen. 16:1-14 and 21:9-19) than the interpretations offered by white male scholars.

The Bible was written by men in patriarchal societies, and from a feminist perspective many biblical passages remain problematic even when divested of their layers of historical interpretation. However, feminist scholars are also demonstrating that the Bible is a multi-faceted collection which invites diverse interpretations. Its ambiguities and apparent contradictions sometimes militate against human equality and freedom, but its central theme is that of a God who has a special concern for the little people, the *anawim*, of history.

Elizabeth Schüssler Fiorenza's work has had a formative influence on feminist biblical studies. Fiorenza studies the New Testament in its historical and social context, to reclaim the roles played by women in the early church. She argues that women were considerably more influential as disciples, deacons and leaders than is recognised today, and she seeks to identify scriptural texts which have a liberating message for women, claiming that only these are suitable for use in liturgy and worship.

Phyllis Trible focuses on textual analysis rather than contexts of interpretation. She shows that some key Old Testament narratives, such as the story of Adam and Eve, when re-read in close fidelity to the Hebrew text, expose how androcentric readings and patriarchal ideologies have obscured the text's original meaning.[66]

Women of colour and Third World women bring new questions to bear on readings which have been largely unchallenged by white western Christianity, and the revelations they offer are challenging and surprising. Take, for example, the story of Hagar, Sarah, Ishmael, Isaac and Abraham in Genesis 16:1-15 and 21:9-19.

In the Genesis text, Sarah is infertile so she sends Abraham to conceive a child with her servant, Hagar. But Sarah is consumed by jealousy of Hagar and her son, Ishmael, and when Sarah gives birth to Isaac, she tells Abraham to send Hagar and Ishmael into the wilderness. Sarah, Abraham and Isaac have been key figures throughout Christian history. In Galatians 4:21-5:1, Paul contrasts children born of the free woman, Sarah, with children of the slave woman, Hagar, seeing the former as the church and the latter as the old

Jerusalem. Thus from the earliest days, Christians have interpreted this story as one of Sarah's privilege, and Hagar's exclusion. But womanist theologians such as Williams see in Hagar a symbol of sisterhood for black Christian women who have been enslaved and oppressed by white women as well as by men. Hagar is an Egyptian slave who is abused by her owners and cast out into the desert to fend for herself and her child. But God cares for Hagar and Ishmael, and moreover, Hagar is the only person in the Old Testament to whom is attributed the power of naming God when she says, 'You are El Roi.' (Gen. 16:13). Williams writes, 'Hagar, like many black women, goes into the wide world to make a living for herself and her child, with only God by her side.'[67]

Mukti Barton, an Indian theologian, offers a different interpretation of Hagar and Sarah in her study of women in Bangladesh, where most of the population is Muslim. Muslims trace their religious genealogy through Hagar, Abraham and Ishmael rather than through Sarah, Abraham and Isaac, so the story provides a point of encounter between Muslims and Christians. But in the present global economy, Barton also identifies Sarah with white western feminists, and Hagar with poor Bangladeshi women. She writes:

> If the narrative of Hagar is compared to the current international power struggle, a Bangladeshi woman can be seen as Hagar and her Euro-American sister as Sarah. A Bangladeshi woman can easily be identified as the gentile slave, because she too is dispossessed on account of her ethnicity and economic and political standing as well as her gender. Nationally and internationally a Bangladeshi woman is the exploited one. Sarah is also under the constriction of patriarchy, but she is not dispossessed in every sense. [...] Just as the biblical Hagar could gain nothing by identifying with Sarah as long as Sarah remained the oppressor, so Bangladeshi women cannot possibly benefit from connecting with western feminists until racial, economic and political divisions are acknowledged as clearly as gender issues in their feminism.[68]

While womanist and Bangladeshi representations of Hagar are motivated by the same sense of identification with a woman victimised by patriarchy because of her gender, her ethnicity and her social status, their different theological contexts give rise to different interpretations and emphases.

Mary

Marina Warner, in her influential book, *Alone of All Her Sex*, wrote of Mary that 'the reality her myth describes is over; the moral code she affirms has been exhausted'.[69] Since then, Marian theology and devotion have received new impetus from different sources, not only among conservative Catholics but also (and with a somewhat different emphasis!) among feminist Christians of all denominations. It must be acknowledged, however, that in most Catholic countries devotion to Mary still serves to pacify rather than to empower women. Tissa Balasuriya's controversial book, *Mary and Human Liberation*, argues that traditional Mariology has perpetuated the oppressive and imperialistic tendencies of western patriarchy by cultivating passivity and conformity among colonised peoples.[70]

The task of feminist Mariology is twofold:

We must name, and liberate ourselves from, the destructive effects of 2,000 years of male interpretation of Mary.

We must return to the Scriptures as women within our own cultural contexts, to rediscover the Mary who is liberated and liberator.

The Magnificat emerges as the most powerful focus of our reflection on Mary. Mary announces the reversal of the present order. We must take this challenge seriously. The first reversal must be to rescue Mariology from the control of Catholic male celibates, and hear the voices of women, both Protestant and Catholic, as we observe the mother of Jesus. Mary is also the mother of all and of all Christian traditions, so it is the combined task of women of all traditions to redefine her.

If we recognize that Mary is a woman of the poor, we must also challenge the lie that depicts her as jewelled and elaborately dressed. Because the good news of the Magnificat is bad news for the rich, we reject Mary's hijacking by a wealthy Church – for the consolation of the rich. This simply reinforces the oppression of the poor. If we understand the virgin birth as the beginning of a new order, in which patriarchy can no longer be the basis of human life, we must hear the angel's greeting, 'Hail, full of grace,' as addressed to all of us. We too must participate in changing oppressive relationships and cultural symbols – overcoming patterns of domination and subordination between north and south, rich and poor, male and female, black and white.[71]

Extract from Summary Statement on Feminist Mariology, produced at a conference of Asian Christian women in Singapore in 1987.

There is a growing recognition that the patriarchal representation of Mary is open to challenge, and that she can be seen as a liberating symbol of womanhood. Although she has been held up as a perfect example of feminine submission, passivity and obedience, when women look at Mary through feminist eyes they see a different picture. She is a poor woman of vision and courage, chosen to be the mother of God's Son. In their book, *Mary, Mother of God, Mother of the poor*,[72] Ivon Gebara and Maria Clara Bingemer portray Mary as one who has transcended her own life to become a person who lives not just in history but also in God, in such a way that she acquires universal significance. Thus they emphasise the historical relevance of Mary of Nazareth as a woman who experienced the struggles, joys and griefs of women's lives, while respecting her symbolic significance as one who reveals the mystery and power of God.

Liberation theologians interpret Mary's Magnificat as a protest against the structures of injustice and a powerful affirmation of God's preferential option for the poor. While Christian theology has tended to interpret key events in the Gospel in terms of their spiritual significance, poor people see the harsh realities and political struggles of their own lives reflected in the story of Mary and Jesus. Mary is the poor mother who gives birth in squalor. She is the refugee who must flee with her husband and baby to escape the marauding power of Herod's army. She is the mother who watches the torture and death of her son who is killed because he does not conform to the religious and political authorities of his time. For many people in the world today, these situations are as real as they were 2,000 years ago. One woman from El Salvador describes how she discovered the death of her son:

> I often think of Mary: I suffered so much when they arrested my son. When I went to ask where he was, they said they didn't know. I searched and searched, but couldn't find him. Finally, his corpse appeared, his head in one place and his body in another. I fainted when I saw him. I thought of how the Blessed Virgin also suffered when they told her that her son had been arrested. Surely she went searching for him and later saw him die and buried him. That is why she understands my sorrow and helps me to go on.[73]

David Tombs argues that Latin American women are beginning to challenge the cult of *marianismo* which 'is the female foil to male *machismo*. [...] The *marianista* woman is the long suffering partner of the *machista* man.'[74] He cites the example of the CoMadres of El Salvador, who brought the mothers of the disappeared together in political activism, with Mary as a source of inspiration and spiritual sustenance. In Argentina, Las Madres de Plaza de Mayo also gathered in political protest against the disappearance of the nation's children, and again Mary provided a symbol of maternal power and solidarity. So without denying the continuing difficulties of the marian tradition for women, important new images of Mary are emerging as women begin to find a voice.

Another aspect of the marian tradition is only now beginning to emerge as a significant focus for feminist theology, and that is the association between Mary and creation in the Catholic tradition, in which Mary represents the perfection of the new creation in Christ. Sarah Jane Boss argues: 'In Christian theology and devotion, Mary stands for creation in relation to the Creator. More particularly, she stands for creation in what it is supposed to be its right relationship with the Creator.'[75] Boss suggests that changes in humanity's relationship with nature and in gender relations are reflected in changing images of Mary, so that a society which expresses its human and material relationships in terms of domination and control will have an image of Mary as a woman dominated and controlled by the male God. Yet Boss argues that:

> Against a culture which is set against nature, and in which all flesh is meaningless, the Mother of God is still able to proclaim God's presence within the blood and the milk, the cells and the atoms, of the material creation, and in this [...] she constitutes a potential point of subversion of the present social order.[76]

Creation

An important task for women theologians is to explore the interdependence between nature and culture, between the human body and the rest of creation. In the western tradition, women have been identified with the body, nature and the non-rational, while men have been identified with the spirit, culture and the rational. This reveals a dualistic way of thinking, in which body/nature/woman tend to be regarded as inferior to spirit/culture/man. Some argue that the result has been the development of a society in which men, identified with rationality and order, have taken control of women's bodies and nature, identified with non-rationality and disorder. Moreover, Christian theology has had a tendency to identify creation with femininity, and God with masculinity. This tendency has recently been dogmatically reasserted in Roman Catholic teachings, so that the defence of the male priesthood focuses on a cluster of beliefs around the fatherhood of God and the essential masculinity of Christ and the priesthood, and the maternal femininity of Mary, creation and the church.

Such ideas present a complex challenge to feminist theologians. They exclude women from positions of authority. They align women with domesticity and motherhood, attributing to them a greater capacity for feeling and a lesser capacity for reasoning than men, while men have appropriated the task of organising culture and ruling the public domain.

But some would argue that insofar as the female body menstruates, gestates, gives birth and nurtures, there is a bond between women and nature which might inform an ecofeminist awareness of the interdependence of all creation. Moreover, the metaphors used to describe nature and the earth in western culture have been predominantly those of maternal and female embodiment. While in medieval Christianity this entailed reverence for the maternal power of nature, in the scientific revolution of the 17th and 18th centuries writers such as Francis Bacon used images of sexual penetration and rape to describe the relationship between science and nature. The shift from a religious to a scientific worldview was therefore accompanied by the objectification and denigration of nature, personified as female.

Some see Christianity as being deeply implicated in the West's continuing abuse and exploitation of the natural world.[77] Others suggest that while this tendency has been present since the early church's destruction of paganism and its denial of the sacred power of nature, it was the scientific revolution that paved the way for the triumph of a masculine value system, the conquest of feminised nature, and the environmental devastation we see today.[78] Either way, Christian ecofeminists seek a new holistic understanding of the relationship between humankind and the rest of creation, informed by the affirmation of a life-giving bond between women and nature, and finding expression in an environmental politics of resistance and struggle on behalf of the poor. Aruna Gnandason, an Indian theologian, writes:

Every struggle of women, particularly women in the periphery of society – Dalit women, tribal women – is a struggle for life. When women 'hug' the trees in the Chipko Andolan, defying the contractors to saw; or when they camp around a nuclear installation, as in the United Kingdom; or when they engage in sustainable agriculture as in Brazil; or when they participate in reforestation programs as in the Green Belt movement in Kenya; or when they struggle against invasive reproductive technologies and other medical technologies that colonise women's wombs; or when they work against the Narmada Valley project of dams – they do all these things because of women's deepest longing to affirm life.[79]

For Christian women, this longing to affirm life is expressed and nurtured in liturgical and sacramental celebrations. But usually these are the carefully guarded and controlled domain of a male hierarchy. How do women bring a liberative vision to Christian worship, and how might this lead to the creation of a more inclusive and joyful understanding of church?

Sacraments and liturgy

Christian feminists often find that they struggle most intensely with feelings of alienation and exclusion in times of worship. Women are expected to pray to a father God as sons and brothers, to recite creeds in which all are described as men, to accept that 'man embraces woman' while knowing full well that there comes a point where that is no longer true, where man excludes woman and refuses her any participation in his functions of priesthood and leadership. In these circumstances, it can be a weekly struggle to stay, to pray and to trust that, in the words of Julian of Norwich, 'all manner of things shall be well'. But things are changing, and many women find it possible to achieve a balance between participation in traditional and often male-defined acts of worship, and an exploration of other forms of worship which allow women to come before God in a celebration of difference and womanliness. How does this lead to a feminist-liberationist understanding of the sacraments and worship?

Mananzan refers to 'the anguish of awareness'[80] when in the 1970s she found herself catapulted from a period of theological studies in Europe, into participating in strikes and rallies alongside the workers of the Philippines.

She writes of the struggle to integrate her faith with her new level of social awareness, and how this affected her spirituality. She uses the language of a dark night of the soul, leading to a *metanoia* or conversion, which finally found expression in an exuberant feminist spiritual awakening. She writes:

> The release of creative energy and the new insights in the women's struggle have [...] affected a new focus and new expressions of spirituality. It is creation-centered rather than sin- and redemption-centered. It is holistic rather than dualistic. It is risk rather than security. It is a spirituality that is joyful rather than austere, active rather than passive, expansive rather than limiting. It celebrates more than it fasts; it lets go rather than holds back. It is an Easter rather than a Good Friday spirituality. It is vibrant, liberating, and colourful.[81]

This desire to express joy and delight is perhaps surprising, given that feminist spirituality often emerges from a dark backdrop of struggle and even loss of faith. Yet it is a common theme in women's spiritual writings. Maybe women recognise more effectively than some male liberationists that there is 'a time for tears, a time for laughter; a time for mourning, a time for dancing.' (Eccl. 3:4) Some have suggested that one significant problem of liberation theology in Latin America might be in part due to its politicisation of worship, so that people whose weekly lives were a constant political struggle found that Sundays merely offered more of the same. Feminist spirituality might offer a way of reconciling a passionate commitment to justice with the liberating joy of worship for its own sake, or for the sake of a God who is intimately one with but also infinitely greater than all human concerns.

Something of this sense of the intimacy and the infinity of God is suggested in Bingemer's moving description of the eucharist, which describes this most important symbol of the Christian faith in metaphors of the maternal body. Bingemer suggests a path ahead which mother church might tread, if only she dares to follow the way that women are showing her.

Throughout Latin America, in the rural areas and the poor districts on the edges of cities, there are millions of women conceiving, bearing, and suckling new children of the common people. Sometimes they do it with difficulty, pain, and suffering, sometimes with the last trickle of life left in them. This female body, which is extensive and multiplies in other lives, which gives itself as food and nourishes with its flesh and blood the lives it has conceived, is the same body that wastes away and dies tilling the earth, working in factories and homes, stirring pans and sweeping floors, spinning thread and washing clothes, organizing meetings, leading struggles, chairing meetings, and starting singing. It is the woman's body, eucharistically given to the struggle for liberation, really and physically distributed, eaten and drunk by those who will – as men and women of tomorrow – continue the same struggle of patience and resistance, pain and courage, joy and pleasure. Breaking the bread and distributing it, having communion in the body and blood of the Lord until he comes again, means for women today reproducing and symbolising in the midst of the community the divine act of surrender and love so that the people may grow and the victory come, which is celebrated in the feast of true and final liberation.

From: María Clara Bingemer, 'Women in the Future of the Theology of Liberation' in Marc H. Ellis and Otto Maduro (eds.), *The Future of Liberation Theology – Essays in Honour of Gustavo Gutiérrez*, Orbis Books, Maryknoll, 1989, p486.

Conclusion:
A chorus of whispers

The voices represented here are a chorus of whispers which do not amount to a great global movement. Although their visions are informed by a universal quest for justice, peace and the integrity of creation, they belong within the movement broadly known as postmodernity, with its disintegration of historical grand narratives and its plethora of different voices arising from a multitude of social contexts. But while postmodernity can mean a descent into the abyss of nihilism and unredeemed materialism, it can also be a moment of opportunity for those whose stories have been excluded from the telling of history. Johann-Baptiste Metz uses the term 'dangerous memories' to refer to these alternative versions of history which threaten discourses of power and domination.

Women's theologies are made up of memories and hopes which are dangerous to those who have an investment in the prevailing order. That is why they are rarely welcomed by those in positions of authority, whether in the church or in secular institutions. But liberation theologies can also be threatening to the poor who depend upon the paternalism of the rich. Nagle shows how liberation movements create complex fractures in society, with men and women, rich and poor, clergy and laity, forming alliances on both sides. He uses the term 'the anthropology of insecurity' to explore how 'Liberation theology stepped into, and heightened, a controversy that touched on the most fundamental elements of life in a deeply insecure part of the world'.[82]

Does opposition to feminist-liberationist movements come only from those who are stakeholders in the present system? Might it not also come from poor people themselves, whose voices are appropriated and whose interests are distorted by theologians? To what extent do the feminisms explored here constitute liberating movements of and for poor women, and to what extent are they the products of a western-educated theological elite remote from the realities of women's lives?

Most of the women I have quoted are educated theologians who might not experience at first hand all the struggles of those they write about, but all put their theology at the service of the poor. For some, their lives and freedom are under threat. Some Roman Catholic feminists such as Ivone Gebara and Lavinia Byrne have suffered repeated harassment from the Vatican. For nearly 2,000 years, conservative forces in the church have primarily been concerned to silence women and restrict their access to theological education and leadership. They do not easily accept that women might have something significant to say to the people of God.

Women's theological visions attest to a new awakening among Christians. If such visions pose a fundamental challenge to the worn out structures of an archaic institution, they also offer rebirth and transformation. They serve as a reminder of how spiritually impoverished western society has become, and how the spiritual wealth of the materially poor might yet be our guide as we grope our way towards a more holistic way of being and knowing. But as so many of these writers point out, until we in the West are willing to relinquish our domination of the world's resources, we will never be able to claim solidarity with those who beg outside the gates of our global banqueting halls, nor perhaps with the Lord who hears the cry of the poor.

A healing touch

Who touched me? Somebody touched me
With the needs, the dreams and the hopes of the world
Who touched me? Somebody touched me
And I turned and saw the people
And I turned and listened to their story
Who touched me? Somebody touched me
And I turned and saw two worlds where God created one
And the gates of the rich were closed

And I dreamed of the world you created
A garden with plenty for everyone
With a stream of clean flowing water
For all to drink

And I believe in life
I believe in hope
I believe in a future where there is one world
Which we build together.
Who touched me? Somebody touched me
And I pray
Stay with us, Lord, as we work for a better world.

Amen.

Linda Jones (CAFOD)[83]

Notes

1   Noeleen Heyzer, Director of UNIFEM (United Nations Development Fund for Women), Plenary Address to the Fourth World Conference on Women, quoted on UNIFEM website, www.unifem.undp.org.

2   *Progress of the World's Women 2000* – a report examining the progress of the world's women from the mid 1980s to the late 1990s, on www.unifem.undp.org.

3   Gerda Lerner, *The Creation of Feminist Consciousness from the Middle Ages to Eighteen-seventy*, Oxford University Press, New York and Oxford, 1993, p vii.

4   See Catherine M. Scott, Women, *Faith and Empowerment*, MA dissertation, University of East Anglia, 1997.

5   Cf. John Milbank, 'The End of Dialogue' in Gavin D'Costa (ed.),*Christian Uniqueness Reconsidered: The Myth of a Pluralistic Theology of Religions*, Orbis Books, Maryknoll NY, 1990.

6   Andrew Brown, 'Hume? A Czech? Or an Undry Martini?' in *The Spectator*, 25 April 1998, p14.

7   Nikki van der Gaag, 'Women: Still Something to Shout About' in *New Internationalist*, August 1995, p9.

8   See Angela West, *Deadly Innocence: Feminism and the Mythology of Sin*, Cassell, London and New York, 1995.

9   Robin Nagle, *Claiming the Virgin: The Broken Promise of Liberation Theology in Brazil*, Routledge, New York & London, 1997, p161.

10 See Alan Thomas *et al*, *Third World Atlas*, second edition, Open University Press, Buckingham, 1994, p61.

11 Figures taken from *New Internationalist*, August 1995, pp 18-19, and January/February 1998, pp24-25.

12 Special Correspondent, All Africa News Agency, 'Somalia: No Let Up For Women in Situations of Conflict', June 12, 2000 at *Africa News Online*, www.africanews.org.

13 Ferial Haffajee, 'Women Peace It Together' in Flame/Flamme, 25 November 1999, at *Africa News Online*, www.africanews.org.

14 Figures taken from *New Internationalist*, August 1995, p18.

15 Quoted in 'Help Break the Silence,' leaflet produced by The Women's Co-ordinating Group for Churches Together in England.

16 See the report by Ferial Haffajee, 'Women Have Little to Celebrate' in *The Nation* (Nairobi), June 10, 2000, at *Africa News Online*, www.africanews.org.

17 *Ibid.*

18 Figures taken from *Developments*, Issue 1, First Quarter 1998, published by Department for International Development (DFID), p29.

19 Quoted in a press release prepared by Catholics for a Free Choice (CFFC), March 15, 2000, on seechange.org.

20 Annabel Miller, 'The Holy See in the Public Square' in *The Tablet*, 23 September 1995, p1192.

21   See 'Head of Vatican Delegation Looks at Beijing Conference: Remarks made by Mary Ann Glendon' on www.catholicity.com.

22   Patricia Stoat, letter to *Network*, journal of the Catholic Women's Network, Summer Issue, No. 63, June 2000, p19.

23   Mercy Amba Oduyoye, 'Poverty and Motherhood' in A. Carr and Elisabeth Schüssler Fiorenza, *Concilium – Motherhood: Experience, Institution, Theology*, T & T Clark, Edinburgh, 1989, pp23-4.

24   Pope John Paul II, *Evangelium Vitae*, 1995, n99.

25   See William Oddie, *What Will Happen to God? Feminism and the Reconstruction of Christian Belief*, SPCK, London, 1984.

26   Urvashi Butalia, 'Domestic murder and the golden sea' in *New Internationalist*, January/February 1999, p20.

27   For examples of these and other women's theologies, see Ursula King (ed.), *Feminist Theology from the Third World: A Reader*, SPCK/Orbis Press, London/Maryknoll, 1994.

28   Ivone Gebara, 'Women Doing Theology in Latin America' in Elsa Tamez (ed.), *Through Her Eyes: Women's Theology from Latin America*, Orbis Books, Maryknoll, 1989, pp39-41.

29   Ursula King (ed.), *Feminist Theology from the Third World*, p11.

30   *Ibid*, p12.

31   *Ibid*. This expression was used by the Ghanaian woman theologian, Mercy Amba Oduyoye.

32   Ecumenical Association of Third World Theologians, 'Final Document: Intercontinental Women's Conference' (Oaxtepec, Mexico, 6 December, 1986) in Alfred T. Hennelly (ed.), *Liberation Theology: A Documentary History*, Orbis Books, Maryknoll, 1990, pp514-6.

33   Nagle, *Claiming the Virgin, op cit.* p160.

34   Marigold Best and Pamela Hussey, *Life out of Death: The feminine spirit in El Salvador*, CIIR, London, 1996, p6.

35   *Ibid*, p7.

36   Ivone Gebara, 'The Face of Transcendence as a Challenge to the Reading of the Bible in Latin America' in Schüssler Fiorenza, Elisabeth (ed.), *Searching the Scriptures, Volume 1, A Feminist Introduction*, SCM Press, London, 1993, p173.

37   Ana María Bidegain, 'Women and the Theology of Liberation' in Tamez (ed.) *op cit*, p29.

38   Quoted in Kwok Pui-lan, 'Asian Feminist Theology: The Dream of Sun Ai Lee-Park' in *In God's Image*, Vol. 18, No. 3, 1999, p33.

39   Yvonne Dahlin, Maria Klasson Sundin and Margareta Koltai, 'In Memory of Sun Ai Lee-Park' in *In God's Image*, Vol. 18, No. 3, 1999, p21.

40   Aida Jeannie Nacpil-Manipon, 'Global Trends and Asian Women: Of Saints and Icons in the Time of Globalisation' in *In God's Image*, Vol. 17, No. 1, 1998, p12.

41   Figures in this section are taken from news reports posted on the website, www.captive.org.

42   Marianne Katoppo, 'The Church and Prostitution in Asia' in King (ed.), *op cit.*, p116.

43   For further information, contact Purple Rose Campaign Secretariat, GABRIELA, No. 35 Scout Delgado St., Bgy. Laging Handa, Quezon City, Philippines, e-mail gab:@mnl.sequel.net.

44   See dalitchristians.com/dalit_christians.htm.

45   See www.dalits.org/Blackpaper.html.

46   Swarnalatha Devi, 'The Struggle of *Dalit* Christian Women in India' in King (ed.), *op cit.*, p136.

47   See the video about Chung Hyun Kyung, *Gentle But Radical*, produced by the World Council of Churches, Geneva.

48   Extract taken from King, *op cit.*, pp392-4.

49   Chung Hyun Kyung, *Struggle to be the Sun Again: Introducing Asian Women's Theology*, SCM Press, London, 1991, p113.

50   *Ibid.*

51   Cf. Emmanuel Martey, *African Theology: Inculturation and Liberation*, Orbis Books, Maryknoll, 1993, pp74-5.

52   See UNAIDS: Press Release 2000 on www.unaids.org.

53   Daisy N.Nwachuku, 'The Christian Widow in African Culture' in Mercy Amba Oduyoye, and Musimbi R.A. Kanyoro (eds.), *The Will to Arise – Women, Tradition, and the Church in Africa*, Orbis Books, Maryknoll, p63.

54   See Elizabeth Amoah, 'Femaleness: Akan Concepts and Practices' in Jeanne Becher (ed.), *Women, Religion and Sexuality*, WCC Publications, Geneva, 1990, p147.

55   Sara C. Mvududu, 'Revisiting Traditional Management of Indigenous Woodlands' in Rosemary Radford Ruether (ed.), *Women Healing Earth. Third World Women on Ecology, Feminism and Religion*, SCM Press, London 1996, pp43-60.

56   Alice Walker, *In Search of Our Mothers' Gardens: Womanist Prose*, The Women's Press, London, 1985, pxi.

57   *Ibid*, pxii.

58   *Ibid.*

59   Katie Geneva Canon, 'Moral Wisdom in the Black Women's Literary Tradition' in Judith Plaskow and Carol P. Christ (eds.), *Weaving the Visions: New Patterns in Feminist Spirituality*, HarperSanFrancisco, San Francisco, 1989, p282.

60   Teresa M. Hinga, 'Jesus Christ and the Liberation of Women' in Oduyoye and Kanyoro (eds.) *op cit*, p187.

61   *Ibid*, p191.

62   *Ibid.*

63   Mary John Mananzan, 'Feminist Theology in Asia' in *Feminist Theology*, No. 10, September 1995, p31.

64   David Tombs, 'Crucifixion, State Terror and Sexual Abuse', paper presented at the Society for Study of Theology Annual Conference (Bible and Theology Seminar), April 1999, Edinburgh.

65   Delores S. Williams, 'Black Women's Surrogacy Experience' in Paula M. Cooey, William R. Eakin and Jay B. McDaniel (eds.), *After Patriarchy: Feminist Transformations of the World Religions*, Orbis Books, Maryknoll NY, 1993), pp8-9.

66   See Phyllis Trible, *God and the Rhetoric of Sexuality*, Fortress Press, Philadelphia, 1978.

67   Delores S. Williams, *Sisters in the Wilderness. The Challenge of Womanist God-Talk*, Orbis Press, Maryknoll NY, 1993, p33.

68   Mukti Barton, *Scripture as Empowerment for Liberation and Justice. The Experience of Christian and Muslim Women in Bangladesh*, CCSRG Monograph Series 1, Department of Theology and Religious Studies, University of Bristol, 1999, p137.

69   Marina Warner, *Alone of All Her Sex. The Myth and the Cult of the Virgin Mary*, Picador, London, revised edition 1990 (first edition 1976), p338.

70   See Tissa Balasuriya, OMI, *Mary and Human Liberation – the story and the text*, ed. Helen Stanton, Mowbray, London, 1997.

71   Taken from King (ed.), *op cit*, pp271-4.

72   Ivone Gebara and María Clara Bingemer, *Mary, Mother of God, Mother of the Poor,* trans. Paul Burns, Burns & Oates, Tunbridge Wells, 1989.

73   Quoted in *Celebrating One World – a Resource Book on Liturgy and Social Justice*, CAFOD, St. Thomas More Centre, London, 1989, p95.

74   David Tombs, 'Machismo and Marianismo: Sexuality and Latin American Liberation Theology' in Hayes, M.A., Porter, W. and Tombs, D. (eds.), *Religion and Sexuality*, Sheffield Academic Press, Sheffield, 1998.

75   Sarah Jane Boss, *Empress and Handmaid. On Nature and Gender in the Cult of the Virgin Mary*, Cassell, London and New York, 2000, p13.

76   *Ibid*, p23.

77   See Lynn White Jr., 'The Historical Roots of Our Ecologic Crisis' in Mary Heather MacKinnon and Moni McIntyre (eds.), *Readings in Ecology and Feminist Theology*, Sheed & Ward, Kansas City, 1995.

78   See Carolyn Merchant, *The Death of Nature*, Wildwood House, London, 1982.

79   Aruna Gnanadason, 'Toward a Feminist Eco-Theology for India' in Ruether, (ed.) *op cit*, p75.

80   Mary John Mananzan, OSB, 'Theological Perspectives of a Religious Woman Today – Four Trends of the Emerging Spirituality' in King (ed.), *op cit*, p344.

81   *Ibid*, p347.

82   Nagle, *op cit*, p22.

83   Taken from *Journey to the Millennium and beyond. Reflections, prayers and poems of Christian women*, National Board of Catholic Women, McCrimmon Publishing, London, 1998, p131.

Bibliography

Balasuriya, Tissa OMI, *Mary and Human Liberation – the story and the text*, ed. Helen Stanton, Mowbray, London, 1997.

Barton, Mukti, *Scripture as Empowerment for Liberation and Justice. The Experience of Christian and Muslim Women in Bangladesh*, CCSRG Monograph Series 1, Department of Theology and Religious Studies, University of Bristol, 1999.

Becher, Jeanne (ed.), *Women, Religion and Sexuality*, WCC Publications, Geneva, 1990.

Best, Marigold and Hussey, Pamela, *Life out of Death: The feminine spirit in El Salvador*, CIIR, London, 1996.

Boss, Sarah Jane, *Empress and Handmaid. On Nature and Gender in the Cult of the Virgin Mary*, Cassell, London and New York, 2000.

Chopp, Rebecca S. and Davaney, Sheila Greeve (eds.), *Horizons in Feminist Theology: Identity, Tradition, and Norms*, Fortress Press, Minneapolis, 1997.

Chung Hyun Kyung, *Struggle to be the Sun Again: Introducing Asian Women's Theology*, SCM Press, London, 1991.

Coyle, Kathleen, *Mary in the Christian Tradition From a Contemporary Perspective*, Gracewing, Leominster, 1996.

Daly, Mary, *Beyond God the Father: Towards a Philosophy of Women's Liberation*, The Women's Press, London, 1986, p19.

Ellacuría, Ignacio S.J. and Sobrino, Jon S.J. (eds.), *Mysterium Liberationis. Fundamental Concepts of Liberation Theology*, Orbis Books, Maryknoll, 1993.

Ellis, Marc H. and Maduro, Otto (eds.), *The Future of Liberation Theology – Essays in Honour of Gustavo Gutiérrez*, Orbis Books, Maryknoll, 1989.

Gebara, Ivone and Bingemer, María Clara, *Mary, Mother of God, Mother of the poor*, Burns & Oates, Tunbridge Wells, 1989.

Gutiérrez, Gustavo, *A Theology of Liberation*, revised edition, SCM Press, London, 1988.

John Paul II, 'A Letter to Women' in the *Tablet*, 15 July 1995.

Johnson, Elizabeth A. *She Who Is. The Mystery of God in Feminist Theological Discourse*, Crossroad, New York, 1992.

King, Ursula (ed.), *Feminist Theology from the Third World: A Reader*, SPCK/Orbis Press, London/Maryknoll, 1994.

LaCugna, Catherine Mowry, *God for Us – The Trinity and Christian Life*, HarperSanFrancisco, San Francisco, 1991.

Lerner, Gerda, *The Creation of Feminist Consciousness – from the Middle Ages to Eighteen-Seventy*, Oxford University Press, New York/London, 1993.

MacKinnon, Mary Heather and McIntyre, Moni (eds.), *Readings in Ecology and Feminist Theology*, Sheed & Ward, Kansas City, 1995.

Mananzan, Mary John et al (eds.), *Women Resisting Violence: Spirituality for Life*, Orbis Books, Maryknoll, 1996.

Martey, Emmanuel, *African Theology: Inculturation and Liberation*, Orbis Books, Maryknoll, 1993.

Martin, Francis, *The Feminist Question: Feminist Theology in the Light of Christian Tradition*, T & T Clark, Edinburgh, 1994.

Merchant, Carolyn, *The Death of Nature*, Wildwood House, London, 1982.

Milbank, John, 'The End of Dialogue' in Gavin D'Costa (ed.), *Christian Uniqueness Reconsidered: The Myth of a Pluralistic Theology of Religions*, Orbis Books, Maryknoll NY, 1990.

Nagle, Robin, *Claiming the Virgin. The Broken Promise of Liberation Theology in Brazil*, Routledge, London and New York, 1997.

National Board of Catholic Women, *Journey to the Millennium and beyond. Reflections, prayers and poems of Christian women*, McCrimmon Publishing, London, 1998.

Oddie, William, *What Will Happen to God? Feminism and the Reconstruction of Christian Belief*, SPCK, London, 1984.

Oduyoye, Mercy Amba and Kanyoro, Musimbi R.A. (eds.), *The Will to Arise. Women, Tradition, and the Church in Africa*, Orbis Books, Maryknoll, 1992.

Oduyoye, Mercy Amba, 'Poverty and Motherhood' in A. Carr and, Elisabeth Schüssler Fiorenza, *Concilium – Motherhood: Experience, Institution, Theology*, T & T Clark, Edinburgh, 1989.

Pope John Paul II, *Evangelium Vitae*, Catholic Truth Society, London, 1995.

Rogers, Ted S.J., 'Youth Helping Youth: Peer Education' in *Jesuits and Friends*, Easter 1999.

Ruether, Rosemary Radford (ed.), *Women Healing Earth. Third World Women on Ecology, Feminism, and Religion*, SCM Press, London, 1996.

Ruether, Rosemary Radford, *Sexism and God-Talk – Towards a Feminist Theology*, SCM, London, 1992.

Schüssler Fiorenza, Elisabeth, *But She Said: Feminist Practices of Biblical Interpretation*, Beacon Press, Boston, 1992.

Schüssler Fiorenza, Elisabeth (ed.), *Searching the Scriptures, Volume 1, A Feminist Introduction*, SCM Press, London, 1993.

Scott, Catherine M., *Women, Faith and Empowerment*, MA dissertation, University of East Anglia, 1997.

Tamez, Elsa (ed.), *Through Her Eyes: Women's Theology from Latin America*, Orbis Books, Maryknoll, 1989.

Tombs, David, 'Machismo and Marianismo: Sexuality and Latin American Liberation Theology' in Hayes, M.A., Porter, W. and Tombs, D. (eds.) *Religion and Sexuality*, Sheffield Academic Press, Sheffield, 1998.

Trible, Phyllis, *God and the Rhetoric of Sexuality*, Fortress Press, Philadelphia, 1978.

Warner, Marina, *Alone of All Her Sex. The Myth and the Cult of the Virgin Mary*, Picador, London, revised edition 1990 (first edition 1976).

Williams, Delores S., *Sisters in the Wilderness. The Challenge of Womanist God-Talk*, Orbis Press, Maryknoll NY, 1993.

Other CIIR publications on the church and politics

Guatemala: Never Again!
Interdiocesan Recovery of Historical Memory Project (REMHI)
The Official Report of the Human Rights Office, Archdiocese of Guatemala
Abridged version translated from the Spanish by Gretta Tovar Siebentritt

For the first time in English, the story of Guatemala's civil war as told by its survivors. *Guatemala: Never Again!* is based on some 6,500 testimonies, largely from indigenous Maya, who were the majority among the victims of the country's 36-year conflict. Eye-witness accounts are combined with statistics and analysis to present a rich historical overview of Guatemala over the past four decades.

> 'This searing volume is the martyrology of Guatemala's victims of a brutal war. It is the story of ethnic cleansing in Central America [...] indispensable to anyone who wants to understand the origins of revolution in Latin America.'
> *Robert F Drinan, SJ, Georgetown University Law Center*

CIIR/LAB
1999 ISBN 1899365443 (pbk) 332pp 252x176mm £9.99

Liberation Theology
Coming of age?
by Ian Linden
Comment Series

This concise introduction to liberation theology explains its origins and its fundamental demand that an unjust world should be changed. It explains the evolution of liberation theology in Latin America, the Vatican's opposition to it and the rise of similar religious currents in Asia and Africa. Critiques of liberation theology, particularly from a feminist perspective, are addressed. Its relevance and continued evolution are examined as is its underlying importance for development agencies with Christian roots.

1997 ISBN 1852871865 54pp A5 £2.50
Ian Linden is executive director of CIIR.

Life out of Death
The feminine spirit in El Salvador
Women in conversation with Marigold Best and Pamela Hussey

In this anthology, El Salvadorean women reveal, in their own words, how they are coming to terms with their memories of war, death squads and disappearances, and how they are using them to shape a new theology and work for a better future. Women from Christian communities, women's groups and political organisations show how it is possible, through remembrance, to effect spiritual and physical healing. Their courage and hope are inspirational.

1997 ISBN 185287189X 210pp 215x137mm £7.95

Special offer — the Santo Domingo documents

Santo Domingo Conclusions
Fourth General Conference of Latin American Bishops, October 12-28, 1992
New evangelisation, human development, Christian culture
CAFOD and CIIR

1993 ISBN 1852871210 192 pages 227x152mm £9.99

Santo Domingo and After
The challenges for the Latin American church
by Gustavo Gutiérrez, Francis McDonagh, Cândido Padin OSB and Jon Sobrino SJ

1993 ISBN 1852871202 68pp 214x136mm £6.99

The fourth General Conference of Latin American Bishops was a moment of self-definition for the Latin American church. Coinciding with the 500th anniversary of the arrival of Christianity in the Americas, the conference attempted to evaluate the church's past and map a strategy for the future. Despite a fierce challenge from a conservative minority supported by the Vatican, the bishops reaffirmed the 'preferential option for the poor' and pledged the church to work for the promotion of women and develop a new relationship with indigenous and African American culture. **Santo Domingo Conclusions** contains the conclusions of the conference and other key documents, including messages from Pope John Paul II to the indigenous people and to African Americans. The tension and manipulation surrounding the conference are described in **Santo Domingo and After** by an eyewitness, two leading Latin American theologians and a bishop excluded from the conference by the Vatican.

Buy both books for £11.98, a saving of £5.

Romero
Martyr for liberation
The last two homilies of Archbishop Oscar Romero of El Salvador, with an analysis of his life and work by Jon Sobrino SJ and a preface by Cardinal Basil Hume

The sermons in this book show Romero in action, and the study of his life explains his importance as a model of faith and pastoral ministry.

1982, reprinted 1984 and 1986 ISBN 0946848491 76pp A5 £2.95

Archbishop Oscar Romero
A Shepherd's Diary
translated by Irene B Hodgson, with a foreword by Thomas E Quigley and introduction by James R Brockman SJ

Archbishop Oscar Romero's diary, covering the last 12 years of his life, provides a unique insight into the life and thoughts of one of the 20th century's most important and outspoken religious figures.

CAFOD and CIIR

1993 ISBN 1852871091 542pp 236x152mm (hdbk) £14.99

52